Wisdom

Wisdom

L. Taylor

Copyright © 2010 by L. Taylor

All rights reserved. No part of this book may be reproduced by any mechanical, photographic, or electronic process, or in the form of a phonographic recording; nor may it be stored in a retrieval system, transmitted, or otherwise be copied for public or private use—other than for "fair use" as brief quotations embodied in articles and reviews without prior written permission of the publisher.

The author of this book does not dispense medical advice or prescribe the use of any technique as a form of treatment for physical or medical problems without the advice of a physician, either directly or indirectly. The intent of the author is only to offer information of a general nature to help you in your quest for emotional and spiritual well-being. In the event you use any of the information in this book for yourself, which is your constitutional right, the author and the publisher assume no responsibility for your actions.

Printed in the United States of America

*Dedicated to my faithful
and loving students.
I bow to your Inner Light!*

TABLE OF CONTENTS

Introduction _____ *1*

The Universe Speaks _____ 3
Being Versus Doing _____ 5
Ebb and Flow _____ 7
The Human Experience of Time _____ 9
Religion _____ 11
Intuition _____ 13
Spiritual Awareness _____ 15
Stillness _____ 17
A Flower Among the Rocks _____ 19
Enjoying Life Does Not Make You Weak _____ 21
Let Nature Recharge Your Spirit _____ 23
Rediscovering Purity _____ 25
Spending Time in Devotion _____ 27
The Labor of Becoming _____ 29
Patience as You Grow _____ 31
The Evolution of Humanity _____ 35
Bowing Before Change _____ 37
The Pen of Choice _____ 39
Seeing is Not Believing _____ 41

The Man and the Flood	43
Attending to Your Evolution	47
Hammer, Nails and Truth	49
Words of Encouragement	51
Impatience and the True Nature of Time	53
Feeling Separate	55
Leaves in the Wind	57
Behold—the Truth	59
The Power of Creation	61
What Color are Your Glasses?	63
Embracing Winter	67
Lessons from the Land	69
Raise Your Spear	71
From Trying to Success	73
Shedding Your Spiritual Skin	75
Receive Blessings with Grace	77
The Value of Spiritual Practice	79
A Blessed Holiday Season	81
Ask for Help to Help Yourself	83
Opening to What May Be	85
About the Author	*89*

Introduction

    In 1993, my life changed when I discovered I could hear the voices of Spirit Guides and Angels as They shared messages of wisdom and healing with me. Years of dialogue ensued, culminating in the Divine command to record Their words so others could be uplifted by Their guidance and support, as well.
    The following pages contain just such revelations, demonstrating the encouragement, insight and even humor inherent in the Divine Voice. Blank pages have been included at the end for your convenience in note-taking or indexing especially relevant passages. It is my hope that these directives become as valuable a tool on your spiritual Journey as they have been on mine. Indeed, the wisdom you hold in your hands has changed my life forever.
    May the Universe lift you up through these insights which I have pledged my life to preserve, and which I joyfully share with others open to the Voice of Truth.

L. Taylor
Sedona, Arizona

The Universe Speaks

There are none who can tell you how the Universe speaks, there are only those who can listen. If I were to say to you, "I speak with My mouth," would that be true? Do I not speak with My heart and My Energy, as well? To ask how the Universe speaks is to ask how a butterfly dances or how a lizard slithers and moves—It is what It is. There is no separation between what the Universe is and what It does.

This is why We have been talking to you so much about Being rather than *doing*. In order for each soul to realize its full potential, its need, its *reason* there must be a willingness to let go, a willingness to allow and simply Be.

This kind of surrender is a great struggle for humanity. You spend years of your life struggling away from allowing, striving to avoid surrender. You waste your Energy and your life moving and running away from that which could bring you so much joy and Peace. Everything about you is doing and counting and amassing and stacking up for all to see. But these things are nothing. They mean nothing.

There is only one Truth and that is what you are here to Be. Your purpose here is not to *do*, just like the purpose of a flower is not to do. The purpose of you is to Be: to embody, to expand, to enrich, to enliven, to blossom, to wither—and to grow again.

The doership that you struggle with and that you slip on like oil is a quagmire for you. It holds you back and holds you still and holds you stuck and prisoner to your own mind. There is so much sadness in humanity because of your addiction to doership. This one, this first, this foremost Truth that you are here to Be rather than to do is a challenge for those who live in this Age.

The new Age is the Age of Being. It is an Age of allowing, of expansion and surrender. It is not one of strife and struggle, it is not one of trying, it is hardly even one of learning. It is only about Being, and there is no other way to say it.

Being Versus Doing

Many of you would ask, "How do I learn to Be without sitting around and doing nothing all day?" Understanding a principal with your mind is not the answer here. Being is an experience. It is not something you learn from a book. It is often not something you can experience in the presence of others. Being is explored and encountered in solitude and silence. Being is the art of Oneness. Being is the Ultimate Goal.

Yet, you set up many other goals as if they were superior. You erect three-dimensional objects and create boastful documents that say you are superior to others but all of these, even drawn together as one, do not begin to touch the accomplishment of Being.

How do you learn to Be? Stop *doing* for one! Stop going about at a frantic pace and scheduling every last moment of your day and rushing around as if it mattered. If you seek to do something correctly, the first step is to stop doing those things which are in conflict with your goal.

Yet, your society continues to *do* more and more, thinking that the more they do they will suddenly cease doing. How can you stack sand upon sand and expect there will be nothing when you finish? You will *build* something, you will do something and you will not be Being.

If you are addicted to moving fast and you cannot stop doing all of the time because you are not ready, stop doing some of the time. Then spend a few moments in silence and stillness. Stillness must exist in order for you to truly experience the art of Being. This does not necessarily mean physical stillness, for you can walk and look around you, but practicing the art of inner stillness which is accomplished by the absence of all thought and striving.

Many of you are trapped in the doership of thinking. This is why meditation is encouraged, for it teaches you to experience the suspension of thought. It is like the Sky when there are no clouds and the horizon is vast and clear. This is how the mind becomes when the thoughts are silenced.

Learn to exist in a moment where there is no awareness of time and very little separation from Divinity. As you grow and evolve, you can *do* less of the time and practice inner stillness more of the time. So begin now and do not wait. Learn now the gift of silence. Learn now the gift of stillness and unite with Goodness once more.

Ebb and Flow

All of Reality is part of the constant ebb and flow that characterizes the nature of the Universe. Though all elements are universally equal, in the human experience of linear time there is the feeling that death is "bad" and life is "good." In fact, no part of the Universe is bad. It is all simply in flux. In order for Energy to maintain Its nature of change and movement, It must manifest ebb as well as flow.

The human tendency to consider ebb to be negative is a result of attachment: attachment to an experience, a time or a feeling. This propensity actually inhibits your moving forward into the accompanying flow that is the natural counterpart of the ebb cycle.

The natural cycle of ebb and flow forms the basis of the proverb, "Behind every cloud there is a silver lining." This phrase is a simple snapshot of the ongoing and eternal renewal of the Universe. You could also say, "Behind every flow there is an ebb." It is important to understand that the endless cycle of ebb and flow reflects the natural order of things.

Remember there is never one final moment when the Universe ceases evolving. Rather, Allness is forever demonstrating the ebb and flow of pure Energy and Light. Allness—in Its delight of Itself—chooses to manifest as Energy, which requires ebb and flow to maintain purity. The Universe is constantly changing and shifting. So, too, should you continue to grow, transform and evolve in accordance with your level of spiritual devotion and Understanding.

The Human Experience of Time

Everything around you has a season. Everything on Earth originates at a specific instant and is preceded and followed by certain cycles. This is the natural order of linear time and there is a beauty and a measured predictability about it. As a result, there are certain Laws of Energy that are in place in your reality which cannot be circumvented. One of those is the Law of Evolution.

The Law of Evolution states that certain conditions must preexist in order for other conditions to manifest. This is why humans cannot simply snap their fingers and have abundance come to them. Rather, the Law of Evolution says, "There are some things you will have to do to clear the way to manifest that abundance." This has always been the case and always will be the case because of the confines of linear time.

The human experience is all about time, is it not? "I have some, I have none; I give some, I take…" Your clocks, your watches are some of the greatest follies of mankind. Now the calendar was wise: based on the Sun, it counts time in large quantities and allows you to unite with the cycles of the Earth. But the clock, ah…tiny seconds you count, as if they matter. Why watch you the seconds as they go by? In what second do you plan to accomplish some greatness? Do you put it on your calendar and say, "In this hour between these seconds and those I will accomplish this great task!"

You take time and you try to hold it in your hands or on your wrist. Time is your friend, yet time is your superior. It is what it is without you and still you try to hold it—in its vastness, in its greatness—as if you can control it.

There are some who even seek the appearance of conquering time. "I will change my face," they say, "so that it appears time has no mastery over me!" You tear apart your physical form and you put it back together like a lump of clay and you declare, "Ah, yes, everyone can see that time does not touch me!" But we all know that time touches everyone.

Beyond linear time the concepts of "first" or "best" have no relevance or claim on reality. The ideas of "faster" or "slower" are likewise unimportant. Such things are valid only within the container of human existence and beyond it everything you have come to know of matter and movement, in addition to time and space, completely cease to exist.

For, beyond the human container all limitations cease.

Religion

    Humans, in their ever-continuing search for Understanding and knowledge, are going to eventually ask every single question that can possibly be asked. One of those questions is, "What is God?"
    As civilizations confront questions which cannot be answered, generation after generation continues to grapple with them. They wonder, "Is there life outside this planet? How did the Earth begin? Is there a God?" These kinds of questions have no answers that human minds can understand. Eventually, when seekers cannot put Divinity into an acceptable answer box they start to feel a little uncomfortable. They feel they need to have an answer, so they create one.
    And so humanity says, "God is a man," or "God is a woman." People say, "God walked on the Earth," or "God has never walked on the Earth." This lets individuals choose, it allows them to hand-pick their beliefs and make them up as they go along. Does that make them true? Not necessarily.

Modern human religion has very little to do with the Source or Divine Energy at all. Religion has become a fencing around a person or people that keeps some in, keeps others out, and therefore provides a sense of security. It is a method humans have devised to try to quantify the Source. Conceptualizing the Divine is like trying to hold time or wisdom in a bottle: it cannot be done. So, modern religion typically has more to do with putting things in manageable form for the mind to grasp than with discovering genuine Truth.

There are some people who have it right. Unfortunately for those who like things in "boxes," the people who have it most right are the ones who have no box. This is hard to accept for many but that is, in fact, the Truth about religion. The ones who are willing to see the concept of the Divine as fluid and beyond their understanding, those who can acknowledge that they *know not*, are the ones who are closest to the Truth.

Intuition

    Those of you who experience intuition on a regular basis often find yourselves unable to explain why you feel a certain way or why you make the choices you do. You have no way to prove that the insights you are experiencing are real. You have no way to explain them as "rational" or "logical." Therein lies the problem, and many find it easier to just shut themselves off to intuitive experiences altogether.

    However if you can move past bewilderment and resistance, life can become different for you. You can access a Higher Wisdom and start to move in harmony and unison with the Universe as Its partner, rather than pushing against It.

    You can imagine that instead of standing beside a refreshing river, you could get into the stream and flow with it. Rather than just looking at the powerful water and wondering, "What is this flow about? What does it mean to be guided by my intuition?" you could wade into the water and truly engage your spiritual insight.

Not only do you then start to experience your intuition more frequently first-hand, but it also starts to carry you along. You can essentially learn to step into the water of your abilities and *flow with* them. You may have noticed your intuition once or twice in the past, but perhaps you have never walked into it, waded up to your waist and allowed yourself to fully live from a place of inner Understanding.

If you will grow in the awareness of your natural wisdom, you will find that being in this experience opens you to a larger flow of Energy. Just like a river is only one piece of the larger Earth so, too, your wisdom comprises just one part of your spiritual potential. When you begin to live from a place of intuition and inner guidance, the possibilities for helping others and positively influencing the world around you are limitless.

Spiritual Awareness

Certain areas of the world naturally come to enlightenment faster than others. Some civilizations have borne generations of introspective, philosophical thinkers who instinctively dive deep into the search for Understanding. Yet it is difficult to focus on spiritual Evolution if you are surrounded by people who do not understand why Energy is important. If you are more spiritually-minded then, you will tend to feel different from those around you.

In such cases, surround yourself with those who seek Evolution and who realize that life comprises more than a hand-to-mouth existence. It is meant to be a rainbow of colors and experiences which grow more subtle and profound as you evolve. Interestingly enough, the higher you reside on the vibrational scale, the simpler your outer life will actually become.

As you evolve, you will eventually have to accept that there is more to you than meets the eye. At some point, you will have to acknowledge your limitless nature. This can be an uncomfortable process because accepting your limitless nature means seeing yourself as more than you appear to be. You will find it necessary to embrace some gifts within you which have simply been ignored. Simultaneously, you may be forced to acknowledge talents beyond what you may once have considered humanly possible, such as intuition or clairvoyant abilities.

    Have courage as you seek to discover all that lies within you. Opening to a new depth of spiritual potential can lead you to an entirely new level of personal fulfillment as you journey along your Path.

Stillness

    These trees know the art of Being. In order to stop living with so much worry you have to learn this art of Being, too. For practice, learn to identify a bird by the sound of its voice. You think this has no relevance? You are wrong. Maybe you do not need to know what kind of bird it is, but you need to develop sensitivity so that later you are able to be still and listen when someone speaks to you.

    Feel the breeze on your face. Hear the Voice of the Wind. Be taken in by the richness around you. Notice and admire the shapes of the leaves which provide beauty very few people see; to do so shows that you are growing and learning. Keep opening. Keep watch. Learn to know stillness and the *hush*. Feel the whisper of Earth, Sky and Moon.

    The elders of My people valued silence. Silence showed control of one's emotions. The inner stillness of silence showed patience and respect. It was evidence of thinking before speaking. You do not have to belong to a tribe to live in this way. You can be a living symbol of a time that was once past and is now coming again. People are learning to live again in stillness.

But for most people there are too many things going on. What you do with your time has become too much, too fast and it wastes your Energy on things that do not matter. Your precious life is squandered on pursuits that do not add up in the end, things that do not create within your heart a feeling of value, of purpose.

I strongly encourage you to simplify. Your spirit needs to be simple, quiet and calm. Even within joy and friendship there should be a place of tranquility in the heart. Teach people that the empowerment they seek can come from this quiet, calm center. Remind them that true power does not come from blindly and noisily throwing themselves into circumstances without thinking. True power comes from serious contemplation, looking inward with quiet awareness and stillness, rooted in Being. And from *that* place you act, from that place you move.

Not everyone will understand, but that is not why you are here. You do not live this way for anyone but yourself, for none of us can live the life of our friend. We each have to live our own life and our friends have to live theirs. Learn to hold fast to what you know is right and do not compromise it. You are living this way to honor your Path. And if in the end there is no one there but you, so be it. Rest in stillness and in all that you do allow your Truth to shine.

A Flower Among the Rocks

What you want is what every soul wants, and it is right to want it. Though not easy to get, it is good and natural to want a life of joy and spiritual fulfillment. Your task then is to align and create a reality which supports that desire. Dare to believe that in utilizing your unique gifts you can manifest a life as lovely as any you have ever dared dream possible.

You can create a life that brings you Peace and fulfillment. You can enjoy living your heart's dream, one that honors your spirit's desire and your deepest wish to Commune with Goodness and Light every day. This vision supports your soul's yearning in every way and, yet, you are afraid to step forth and claim it.

But you must commit yourself to it, and the more time you spend nurturing your Path and Purpose the more your life will come to resemble your heart's joyful dream. The answer to creating such a life of fulfillment lies within your Connection to Goodness. That Destiny is waiting, It is before you and you are now ready. Become who you were meant to become.

Everything that has been crying out to be manifest for you is now coming forth in your spirit. It is not too late to create the life that you have held so close in your heart. We can only hope that you will find the courage, the discipline and the dedication to live it.

Look at this flower, growing pink among the rocks. Do you think it worries that it is different? Or does it, by its difference and its tremendous evidence of life, grace this place as lovely? Does it do so with any self-consciousness or fear? No, it simply is. It has mastered the art of Being. That is its job in this experience: to master the art of Being; to be patient, to be fruitful and to wait until the Sun brings it up again in spring when winter has gone.

Learn to be like that. Do not worry about the rocks around you or be concerned with the details of your surroundings. Instead, think of the beauty you may bring to your life and the loveliness you can exemplify by simply Being. Just as you revel in this flower you may never know that somewhere, in an existence you could never understand, walks one who is inspired by your Being, as well.

Enjoying Life Does Not Make You Weak

Some people have the tendency to think that if life becomes too joyful or sweet they will lose their ability to cope when difficulties arise. They are afraid to "let their guard down" and enjoy life's blessings, fearful they will be blindsided by the next challenge life presents.

Do not worry over such things. You have encountered trials before and you have always come out well. Simply because your life has been sweet of late does not mean you should doubt your ability to weather its storms.

In fact, it is partly *because* you have become stronger that your life has become sweeter. You create your reality with your thoughts, intentions and those experiences you contemplate with intense feeling. If you have a dramatic life and you are always thinking about the drama, you will experience even more chaos. Conversely, if life is sweet and all you focus on is the sweetness, you will naturally experience more of the same. Does this mean you should be worried that you will not be able to handle difficulties when next they arise? Absolutely not.

All you have to do is reflect back on a time when you experienced real tragedy. Notice that not only were you able to weather challenge, but you also dug into your Truth and mined the resources of power, drive and perseverance. When difficulties come again you will be able to do the same. Only next time, you will have the ability to simultaneously deepen your spiritual practice, and that will make difficulties even easier to surmount.

So do not worry about what is coming or fear that you will not be able to handle challenges because you have been enjoying a period of Peace and ease. The fact is, you are not who you were before; you are not who you were even a few years ago. There is greater wisdom within you now and you have new ways of dealing with your life. The spiritual sensitivity you have been developing is creating a whole new level of power and awareness within you. When difficulties come, they do not come to the same person they used to. You are a new person now.

Therefore, do not worry so much about your ability to manage future challenges. You will probably do better than you have done in the past even if things are harder, simply because you have been growing so deeply. Walk in the knowledge that your dedication to spiritual evolution will carry you forth with enough power and wisdom to sustain you, regardless of what challenges come your way.

Let Nature Recharge Your Spirit

All the beauty that surrounds you is also within you. If you see the world as lovelier some days, it is because you are lovelier within. The more you are filled with spiritual Truth, the sweeter and more attractive the world around you will appear. There will be more joy, greater beauty and increasing radiance, even in times of challenge. Be aware that when you look around you and see loveliness in things like butterflies with their amazing wings, they are a reflection of you. They are mirroring what you are becoming.

When you notice Nature reflecting your inner beauty back to you, it is because you are a part of Goodness. You are united with the Divine always and everywhere. Allow yourself to receive that Truth. On days when you have a hard time feeling It, seek Our Presence in quiet stillness and We will remind you. This is why it is a good idea for you to spend some time in Nature and meditation every day. In order to feel balanced and in tune with your Highest Truth, you need to take refuge in spiritual practice daily.

You have noticed that your "batteries" go dead and you wind up drained and empty if you do not take time to recharge your spirit. Do not try to avoid this necessary self-care. It is part of the maintenance required to keep your energetic shields strong enough to block out negativity and drama.

You have likewise experienced that if you do not keep your shields strong you are also more accessible to anxiety and fear. So do your spiritual practice, spend time in Nature and let these refuel you. Allow such practices to reignite your fire and reconnect you to Spirit, which is the radiant and powerful essence you truly are.

Rediscovering Purity

Take a moment to recall the purity of your spirit as a child. When you were very young and played among the rocks by the riverbed there was nothing that you needed. You did not seek companionship, you did not crave money, you did not need man-made games. Deep within you there was a sense of contentment, for when the human heart connects with Divinity there is nothing that it needs. As a child you were fulfilled, at peace with Goodness and your Connection to the Great Spirit.

But over time, you were taught to *want* and not to feel satisfied or settled. Just as a little girl learns to brush her hair as her older sister shows, you learned from those around you. You learned fear and self-doubt. You learned worry. You learned to feel separate from Goodness and Spirit. These things you picked up easily because of your natural child's sensitivity. The surrounding environment dictated to you what it deemed appropriate and what it considered good. In that way, every person who dwells in your reality is a byproduct of his or her circumstances.

But these things are not who you truly are, and they are not your True Nature. Your True Nature is the one you remember of childhood Peace: sitting on the ground playing in the grass, crouching in the rocks and finding treasures there…settled, content, joyfully mixing with the Earth. This was a peaceful time for you and, sadly, it did not last. But it can come again.

As a child you had many natural abilities that you are now recalling as an adult. Your attraction to Peace, Truth and Communion is actually part of a spiritual state you worked diligently to create. Likewise, your spiritual sensitivity is a carefully guarded gift you chose not to relinquish upon taking this form. These natural abilities should be celebrated and developed.

Create abundance from your spiritual gifts and you will have the life for which you have always yearned. Begin to open yourself again to who you once were, to the Truth in your heart. Visualize creating a future from the gifts of your spirit and you will find your life as you have always dreamed it to be.

Spending Time in Devotion

For many people, there is some confusion about the nature of Divinity. This bewilderment affects their perception of Truth and their time in devotion.

Long ago you were taught to pray as a supplicant, like a child to a father. Now, as you seek to reconcile yourself to the idea that you are actually a part of the Divine, you are confused. Should you still pray and ask the Divine for things if you, yourself, are a part of It? You wonder if you are just asking *yourself* for something then, and this brings confusion.

There are two things I suggest, and the first is this: continue to spend time in devotion as a way of honoring your Connection to the larger Divinity. Honor your Higher Self as one ray of a larger Sun. Just because you realize you are a part of It does not mean you cannot honor It anymore.

Honoring the Divine is a way to cultivate devotion, which brings you into closer contact with the Universal Energy present all places at all times. Offering up prayer and ritual can still be done with your newfound awareness of your Higher Self as one ray of the Sun because you need not see yourself as a supplicant. Instead, you are cultivating devotion as a way of honoring the greater Energy of which you are a part.

The other reason to spend time in devotion is because it helps you connect to your own inner power very directly. When you move into ritual regularly, you feel your empowered and wise Self. This is an important experience to have on a daily basis. It is wise to use ritual not as a way of looking for answers from outside yourself, but as a way of Communing with the Energy and wisdom of which you are a part.

Then, when it is time for manifesting things in your life, you turn to your Higher Self. You do not need to turn to someone else, you do not have to pray for guidance from an outside source. Rather, you look within your Self, your own Truth, and you find the answers.

As you practice such inner awareness and listening, the experience of finding your own Inner Truth will become easier for you. When it comes time to shine your Light of wisdom and Truth, you will not need to ask anyone else how to do it. You will just shine. As you grow, your discrimination will tell you if you are shining your Light fully and how you can continue to make the most of your inner Truth and wisdom.

The Labor of Becoming

     You are in the process of birthing something. You are re-creating the perception of your small self into an understanding that it is a part of the One Self. As a result, you will be going through the labor pains of *becoming*. When you feel it is difficult for you to keep pace with your accelerating spiritual growth, breathe deeply and center yourself.
     Co-mingle your Energy, every shimmering mote of your Consciousness, with the Allness around you and feel yourself united. To breathe with patient awareness in a moment of pain and confusion—just as any expectant mother would do—is your best course of action. You will start to feel a sweet and soothing Energy help you move through the throes of your spiritual labor.
     This kind of evolutionary labor can last for as many time variations as it takes each mother to deliver a physical child. There is no way to predict how long it will take to become and evolve spiritually. The only thing you can do is deliver yourself completely and wholly unto your transformation.

Do not distract yourself with other things, rather stay focused upon your becoming. Bear in mind that spiritual awakening is the most important birth you can experience and that the process will be expedited by your conscious awareness. So do your best, but remember that in the end you cannot hasten your Evolution beyond the pace that you are capable of maintaining. You can only do so much.

Therefore, as you grow consider yourself thus: kinder and in a gentler way. Regard yourself with greater softness and look upon yourself as one going through a very dramatic, life-altering and sometimes painful shift. The more you can do that, the more easily the process will unfold and the sweeter you will remember your spiritual Journey having been.

Patience as You Grow

The more you yield to the process of spiritual awakening the easier it will be for you. The more you worry or doubt your own capacity to manage it, the slower your process will be. Many of you do not want to grow too slowly and are impatient. But you should know that you are already there, that there is a part of you which has already completed the Journey. There really is nowhere to go because a part of you has already stepped across.

When you acknowledge this more often, and you start to live in concert with that part of you which has already unified with Goodness, then the urge to rush dissolves. You begin to understand that there is no need to go anywhere or do anything. There is nowhere to be but here because there *is* nowhere but here, and there is no time but *this*.

I encourage you to look at the Earth around you and find strength in those things of Harmony and Light. When you attune to the Earth and know Its Peace, you will sense that you have nowhere go. You will feel that you are perfectly where you should be and everything is right on time. The more you return to that Understanding, the sweeter your life will become.

Sometimes spiritual Evolution can feel as if you have been sliced into a million sheets of thin translucence with some parts reveling in complete awareness while others languish in the lowest levels of suffering. Your job is to unify them all and to slowly gather those pieces of yourself together.

Think of them like ducklings. Think of how a baby duckling is soft and fragile. If you were to take a group of tiny ducklings and try to usher them across a gravel road you would have to be very careful, wouldn't you? It would be important not to push them because you could hurt them. You would gently guide them across and they would have to take their time. Their footing would be unsure, and they would "peep" and make a ruckus along the way; some of them would turn around and go the wrong direction and in the end, your Compassion would be your delight. Eventually they would all cross if you attended to them with loving care.

Likewise, all of the lost or lonely aspects of your heart should not be the subject of criticism and impatience. On days when you are prone to frustration, look upon your struggling pieces as little stray ducklings that need a guiding hand. You may wish to use the gentle, guiding hand of a centering breath, soothing music or holding a beloved pet. Such things can help bring those misguided and wandering pieces back onto the path of positive Energy and Peace.

If attended to lovingly, the process of spiritual growth gains momentum and will continue to do so. Feel yourself moving closer to a more complete awakening, open to the joy of it and acknowledge with confidence your ability to attain spiritual freedom. Like our tiny flock of ducklings you will all get there. There are none who are too lowly, for if you have taken human form you are capable of Evolution. So be at peace and know that even the least of these will one day return to the Source.

The Evolution of Humanity

Most of the suffering encountered by humans is the result of an unenlightened, limited view of Reality. It is based on the idea of *a* God, *some* where, noticing or being affected by *you*. This idea of Goodness as a separate entity somewhere watching and judging you is a painful one, indeed.

The reality is all things are Goodness, so God is not separate from anything else and therefore It cannot be accurately conceptualized as singular. There is no "somewhere else" because there is only This Place, and all things are in the same place in the same time—all things are One—so there is no "somewhere else" for Divinity to be. And there is no "pleasing" because that Goodness is in perfection in the non-time that is Now so It cannot be altered. Therefore, It does not feel your actions with pleasure or pain. It knows only Its own perfection and you, too, when you realize you are one with Goodness will know only perfection, yourself.

You ask how long it is going to take for humanity to shift into this new Understanding. In turn I ask you, how long did it take the first time? How long ago was it that your societies embraced philosophies which revered everything as One and all things united and connected? It will presumably take that long again for the human heart to accept a new way of thinking and find within itself a willingness to relinquish its limited concept of Divinity.

You are on the forefront of such a shift in the human perception of Reality. You are pioneers of that new perception. This is the beginning of an entirely new Age and you are truly standing on the dividing line which marks the end of the old and the beginning of the new. Your uniqueness is that you get to look into both. You have lived through the change of a century which has symbolically shown you what it means to experience two parts of a singular Reality. And so will it continue to be.

You will continue to watch as the old concept of Divinity based on fear and judgment diminishes and slowly shifts. You will bear witness as the new becomes a twinkle in the eye of some and is summarily rejected by others. You will watch as humankind chooses the Path it will take. There is no question as to where you will end up eventually, the only question is how long will you take to get there?

Bowing Before Change

When you look around at the trees swaying in the breeze, you are reminded that things in Nature bow. There is nothing in Nature that does not bow to a Higher Energy at some moment; even rock must fall. But the joy of Nature bowing is that when It does, It is transformed into something greater. When ice bows to the Sun, it becomes a stream and is free. When water bows to heat, it becomes mist and is free. When the human form bows to death, it becomes spirit and is free.

And so you, too, will bow before change and it will free you. What is negative about transformation when you realize it brings liberation? Nothing. Only those who try to control that which cannot be controlled will find fear or pain in change. Only those who try to cling with attachment to that which cannot be held—time in its forms of past, present or future—will suffer.

Therefore, remember this Law: when something bows and is transformed, it is set free. As long as it is bowing to the natural flow, it will be transformed and liberated. This is a Law of Nature and it assures that everything following the flow of Evolution will always continue to grow.

The only time you need be concerned is when you feel you are bowing to something that is not in keeping with your evolutionary Path. In those moments you should reconsider your direction, for it is never too late to rearrange your life or make different choices. It is true that you cannot go back but you can alter your direction, refine your Energy, change your ways.

So keep to the natural flow and you will find everything that makes you bow, everything that forces you to bend in your life, will free you of something. By teaching you to bow, it creates of you something greater than you ever before have been.

The Pen of Choice

"Is the experience of this life real or a dream?" you ask. Some have said, "It is not a dream, it is real," while others say, "It is not real, it is a dream!" In the middle you hesitate, wondering which is the right Understanding.

And so I say to you, it is but a dream in that *you create it* moment by moment! Your life experience is not hard and fast a reality beyond your control. It is, in fact, of your own making.

If it pleases you, you can call it a book that you are, at this very instant, writing with your pen of choice. As you choose, you make a stroke of the pen and thus create your reality. As you choose again and stroke the pen once more, you reality changes with it. Over and over you rewrite and re-script that life which you choose to lead.

Be aware that it matters not if you feel yourself having fallen victim. You are, in fact, still in charge of scripting and penning that life which in this instant you are living, breath by breath.

And so time travels on, and your dream weaves itself into what appears to be reality. From that reality are made moments and memories that will last a lifetime and no more. Then you shall begin again with a new dream in a new place, and you shall create that one too as you wish and see fit.

All that ever has been and shall be is within your grasp to maintain and create. Destroy it, too, if you wish for the dream is yours to construct. And everything about your reality is held up only by the whisper of the breath of your desires.

Therefore, dream those things of Light; dream those things of Peace; dream those things of radiance; dream those things of purity and joy. In so doing you shall find yourself in the midst of All That Is, standing in the sacred and holy place that has become your life. And in that instant, you shall feel round about you the constructs of one extraordinary and enormous moment of grace and Truth.

Seeing is Not Believing

When dogs bark to each other, they are sometimes unable to see one another. Yet there is no denying that they are interacting. In the same way, We are communicating with you all the time and to Us there is no denying the conversations we have. Sadly, because We cannot be physically seen with human eyes, many people do not believe that We are communicating with you at all.

As humans you are uncomfortable when you cannot see things. You struggle with faith when something is not visible and some even feel that if an object is not seen, it is not real. Yet emotions are not seen, death is not seen and wind is not seen, but are not these things real?

Divinity is likewise invisible, and yet It is present. You cannot see It with your eyes but that does not make It any less real. In spite of the human phrase, "I must see it to believe it," Reality is not always determined by what can be detected with the eyes. Truth does not have as much to do with what is visible as it has to do with what is felt with the spirit.

Universal Reality *can* be experienced and felt, but one cannot expect It to always be easily perceived. It takes a deeply knowing heart and a mature soul to discern Truth easily. Reality is determined by what is felt with the spirit; not the emotions, not the mind, but the spirit. In the end, those things which are not felt with the spirit are not True.

Allow yourself to be guided by your spirit more. Learn to sense your way through and trust your intuition as fully as you trust your own eyes. As humans, you have lost the ability to sense your way because you have not practiced it, so you should practice it more often now.

Nighttime is a wonderful time to investigate this in the privacy of your own back yard, but instead you disappear inside your houses at night. You miss the opportunity to feel you way around: to walk a path in the dark with your children, to play hide and seek games by moonlight, to rely on your intuitive senses.

Likewise, in your daily life you can strive to become more sensitive when someone is sharing their feelings with you. Listen to another's deeper words, the Energy which lies beneath the voice and resides in the heart. In such a way you can rediscover your ability to sense the Truth and to perceive the things of Universal Reality, be they seen or unseen.

The Man and the Flood

Once upon a time, there was a great storm which created a flood. As the waters broke through levees and overturned trees, people were forced to flee to higher ground. One man did not leave his home but climbed to the roof of his house and sat, surrounded by the rising waters.

The man turned his face to the sky and prayed, "I know you are there God, so please come and save me. I believe You are all-powerful and I know You can come to my aid. Thank you for hearing my prayer."

Within minutes, a neighbor paddled over in a canoe and called up to the man on the roof, "Climb in and we will paddle to safety together!"

The man responded, "No, I don't need your canoe. I have prayed and I know that God will come and save me."

The neighbor in the canoe shook her head and paddled away to safety.

Hours went by and dusk approached. The man on the roof heard a motor and slowly perceived the outline of a fishing boat trolling among the collapsing houses. The boatman saw the man sitting on his roof and shouted, "When I bring my boat alongside your house, jump in and I will take you to safety!"

The man on the roof called out, "That's OK, I don't need your help. I have prayed that God will save me and I trust He will answer my prayers."

The boatman tried to convince him of the growing danger, but finally had to leave the man behind and move on to find others the save.

Night fell. The man on the roof saw a beam of light coming from the sky and heard the approaching sound of a helicopter scouting the area for survivors in need of rescue. The helicopter pilot, seeing the man on the roof, dropped a ladder down to him. The pilot shouted over his loudspeaker, "Grab the ladder! There's not much time but we can still pull you to safety!"

The man on the roof shook his head and shouted, "I don't need your help! I have prayed to the Almighty and believe that He will come. I know that He will save me!"

Baffled, the pilot and crew turned their aircraft toward the next house and faded into the dark. The man on the house continued to pray as night closed overhead and the storm intensified.

An hour later his house was washed away and he drowned.

The next thing he knew, the man was standing before the Light of Truth. Remembering his final, desperate hours on Earth, he questioned the Light he called God.

"Dear God, I am a pious man. I have always believed in Your presence and mercy. I know that You have no beginning or end. Your power is unlimited and You are able to do whatever

You please by the thinking of a simple thought. You can turn mountains to ash and create worlds by Your will. How is it, then, that in my final hours You did not turn Your grace upon me and rescue me with a blink of Your eye? When I prayed with faith in my most desperate hour, why did You not show Your face and save me?"

And the Light said, "I sent you two boats and a helicopter. What more did you want?"

Attending to Your Evolution

You are recalling a recent airplane journey during which you listened as the airline attendant told you what to do in the event of an emergency. She said, if needed, you should put a little oxygen mask over your face and mouth first, before attending to anyone else's safety. Although you may not have considered it before, the same is true of your spiritual Evolution.

As care-takers, you often become so used to neglecting your own needs that you think any attention you pay yourself or your spiritual Journey is unimportant or even selfish! At some point, however, you will have to accept the importance of defending and aligning with your own Truth and Evolution first.

This does not mean that you do not consider others' feelings or that you are not aware of their viewpoints. Rather, it means that when the time comes to make important choices there is only one reality you can truly uphold, and that one is yours. After that is done, you can then attend to the preferences of those around you.

You see, there is really only one being living in your reality at this time, and that one being is you. No one else can learn your lessons, feel your insights or process your experiences. All of the "someone elses" are like two-dimensional characters in your three-dimensional reality. You can see them and touch them, but you cannot feel their emotions or know their innermost Truths any more than they can know yours.

Does this mean that those people are not experiencing, simultaneously, their own realities? No, they are indeed. But it does not change the fact that within your reality you are still the only character who knows your Truth and can walk your Path.

Therefore, you should always honor, bolster and align with your own Truth first. You must do this because without you, the story is over. When you expire, the story of your life expires and it is done; the last page is turned and the book is closed.

Each person needs to fulfill the High Commission of safeguarding his or her own evolutionary experience first, before taking care of others. You are within this life to evolve, so place high value upon your own spiritual becoming and allow your soul to blossom into power and Truth.

Hammer, Nails and Truth

When you are undertaking a project in your home and you need a hammer or a screwdriver, you go to your toolbox and select a tool to use in your work. As you go about your project, there is never any confusion as to who is the craftsman and who is the implement. It is clear that you are in control of the project and your hammer is just a tool you use to accomplish your task.

In like manner, your life is comprised of circumstances which are essentially tools you selected before arriving to help you learn and grow. Each circumstance is different, just as a hammer is different from a screwdriver, but all are tools which assist in your life project of Evolution and spiritual growth.

Sadly, many of you begin to feel that the tools of learning in your lives—such as career, physical form and relationships—are not just tools but actual parts of yourself. Over time you forget that you are here to accomplish a project of growth and becoming. As you find yourself caught up in the ever-increasing complexity of your life project, you begin to attach more and more to the circumstances of your life which are no more than tools for your spiritual Evolution.

Be aware that such a lack of distinction between your True Nature and your tools is just as inaccurate as it would be to mistake yourself for your own hammer and nails. You know without a doubt that you are not your hammer but, sadly, you often do not know with equal certainty that you are not your body, relationships or career.

When you need to be reminded of your True Nature, turn to the unmarred looking-glass of your own soul. Whether it is through seated meditation or blissful Communion in a forest, such moments provide you with the only accurate reflection of your Truth, which is one of Consciousness and bliss. To remember your true state of being, look into the mirror of spiritual Communion, not at the hammer and nails of your life circumstances.

Be aware, too, that you do not spend nearly as much time in Communion as you do interacting with the people and events of your daily life. You can expect that when you get ideas about who you are from the physical world, you will fall into the old habit of thinking that you are the hammer and nails of your job or relationships. So come again and again before the mirror of spiritual Communion and it will remind you of your Inner Truth. For it is only in Communion that you will see an accurate reflection of your state of being, which is Oneness.

Do not be misled by what appear to be the concrete circumstances of your life. All things around you are, in the end, nothing more than a grand backdrop of tools and props within which you learn your life lessons. Always remember that no matter how attached you are, you will never be just a mind or body any more than you could be just a hammer and nails.

Words of Encouragement

      I am Eagle of the Night and I am with you to encourage you. I provide you with eyes to see greater beauty in the place where you now sit, gazing upon the richness of your Earth. It was not long from Now that I walked this land, too, and I am not without my own remembrances of it.

      As you have felt of late, we each carry our own pain with us as we journey. It is like a heavy stone in a satchel and it is a burden. But it does not deprive you of Truth and it cannot keep you from Light. It only makes you strong. And so it is for all those who have come before you and those who will come after. In order to be strong, burdens must be carried. There is no other way.

      Trust Me when I say that you will step up to this life's challenges. You will look your Destiny in the eye. And even at times when It seems to be glowing red hot with steam radiating from Its nostrils like a dragon, you will step forward and you will fight. You will fight ignorance and you will fight fear and you will win, because that is your Destiny.

I do not have form but still I feel and live. And beyond this moment in time, when these days are but a memory, you will live on, too. Your work here will go with you and carry you to a new place where you will be a powerful and deciding force in the Universe. There is very little else for you to do but follow the Path you, yourself, have laid. And there is no one who can determine Its course but you, with your own heart.

Step forward with courage then, my child, and be not afraid. For I am with you, as all Ascended Seekers who have come before and journeyed long and hard on Their quests are with you. We will never leave your side, not even when you quit this body. We will be with you in Eternity, for we are all One; eventually *all* will arrive.

Be encouraged that every soul who lives upon the Earth will ultimately experience this understanding of Oneness and Light. They will know the Truth as you will know the Truth, they will see the Sun as you see the Sun, and they will *hear My voice* as you do. And we will all be together once more.

Impatience and the True Nature of Time

    Imagine a cloud in the sky above you. Visualize how fluid it would be, how you could see through or even travel through it if you wanted. Its edges would be fuzzy and it could actually morph and change before your eyes.

    This is how time truly is. The linear concept of time that humanity struggles with is not the True Nature of time. If you were to start to see time in the way We do, you might feel less inclined to judge your spiritual progress. If you could remember to see time as it truly is from now on, you could save yourself a lot of pain and self-doubt.

    Even the concept of time is, by definition, limited. The human experience of time does not really exist in the larger Universal Reality beyond your physical form. True Time is like our imaginary cloud: It is fluid, It is changing. It does not have clearly defined or delineated edges. It is of a makeup that has no point of reference in your context of matter; time is not a liquid or a solid. True Time is like an emotion. It can come and go, It can ebb and flow. Time can be a little bit, Time can be a lot.

Even though this is not a concept you can easily wrap your mind around, it is something We want you to remember. When you struggle with frustration or impatience you can refer back to this concept of True Time, which is far beyond the linear time humanity experiences.

For once you understand Time, there need be no sense of hurrying or rushing about your spiritual work. Your Evolution will be completed in the same Here/Now within which you are currently living. That moment and this moment exist simultaneously in the Universal Reality of True Time. The sense that you are sometimes rushing, other times plodding toward a goal is born within the misinterpreted context of linear time.

When you start to feel like you need to rush because there is a goal to be had and you cannot get there fast enough, remember these words. Even if you cannot feel it with your heart, trust Us when We say that all there is is the Now. And when you eventually arrive at your goal, you will be standing in the same Now within which you currently reside.

Therefore, it makes no difference to the "you" in 40 years whether you accomplish a particular goal in three years or ten. All will be resolved at some point. That Now of resolution will be the same Now that you will experience when you are 80, and it is the same Now that you are experiencing in this instant.

So let go of the idea that time is an enemy and be at peace as you grow and evolve. For in the end, and in the truest sense, time is on your side.

Feeling Separate

    Today you are thinking about Divinity and longing for Union with the Great Spirit. But you must remember that the separation you feel from Divinity is only a sense of isolation existing in your mind. It is not a separation in Reality. The idea of separateness is something that you struggle with every day, and addressing it now will help bring you a greater sense of Peace and balance sooner rather than later.

    Look at the way the breeze caresses the trees and you will see a similar relationship. Just as the trees welcome the breeze within their boughs, you should feel Our Presence washing over and through you all the time. Let this be a reminder, for if I am with you any time you call how can you be alone? If you can draw Me to you by the merest thought, there can be no separation.

    When you gaze around and observe Nature in all Its loveliness, try to stop seeing It as separate from you, too. When you notice a positive or lovely thing, consider it to be a part of yourself. Say with satisfaction, "There is a piece of me! There is a piece of my Goodness manifest as beauty nearby. And as I look upon that loveliness and I draw myself close to It, I am reminded that this Divine beauty is not separate from my essence. Indeed, It is a part of me."

In so doing you will begin to feel the presence of Goodness with you more of the time, and your illusion of separation will dissolve into the joy of being connected to the Source each and every day.

Leaves in the Wind

      Today is a beautiful fall day and you can feel change is in the air. Look at how joyfully your little puppy is running through the blowing leaves. She has no worries because she can see you right in front of her. She keeps her eyes on your actions and when she senses things are fine with you, she will look around and continue to play. She is keeping her eyes on the one who feeds her, and so should you be.

      Keep your eyes on the One Who Feeds You, the Divinity which nourishes you. Do not worry about the little "leaves" blowing around: people who gossip, the media, the nay-sayers. Those are all just leaves of distraction fluttering nearby. Since anything which enters your proximity affects your Energy, be diligent in eliminating negativity so it does not become a part of who you are.

      Notice the way your pup runs so freely and allows herself to be just what she is. She does not hold back in any way. There is no sense of pretense, nor does she have any inclination to modify her behavior on the basis of ego. She simply is what she is, and so should it be with you.

As you grow and evolve you will feel less inclined to worry about judgment from others. You will be able to comfortably say, "This is who I am." What a wonderful and joyous thing to anticipate: that as you become more truly yourself, you are also more inclined to accept yourself as you truly are. You will begin to see more readily the gifts you possess and to embrace them without concern for the judgments of others.

You do not want your little puppy to be afraid of harmless leaves swirling around her. You want her to be fearless and brave as she lives and loves her puppy life. So, too, should you be. Keep your eyes on the One Who Feeds You. And let everything else be just so many leaves blowing in the wind.

Behold—the Truth

    It is important that all people become aware they can impact the world around them in powerful and eternal ways. Since there is no way to hide Truth, We often say, "The Destiny you are here to live will be read across your face." It will be revealed in your eyes and your spirit, so there is no point in trying to deny your Truth, whatever It may be.

    Just as there is no point in denying your power and wisdom, it is also useless to deny your pain or anger. If societies were to once again understand it is not unwise to stand up and say, "I wish to fight injustice," or improper to say, "I know the Truth," then you would have very different societies and experiences in your human world.

    But it has not been that way for some time and there is a lack of this kind of Truth. There is a lack of transparency, a lack of the evidence of what is *real* and authentic. For your children this causes a lot of confusion because you do not give them a world of reality. In your very interactions with them you often make up stories that do not reflect what is genuine or honest and they know that.

    If children know nothing else, they know Truth. Adults say that children cannot tell reality from fantasy but, in fact, they see more of Truth than anyone else. Simply ask a child a difficult question about the state of things around them and they will often tell you more than you wish to know. They will openly declare that they see a couple fighting or a person who is lonely and sad. Children may not have the conceptual expansiveness to comment on the state of world affairs, that is true. But they will certainly know if someone is angry or frightened, and they can clearly tell you if a person's energy is a little scary or if it feels alright.

    You have had many people say that they see a radiance in you, something like a spark. You cannot see the way you impact others but you do, and you must trust that this is so, regardless of your perception. Your Destiny will be written upon your face, so let It reveal a life growing toward Peace, empowerment and Truth.

The Power of Creation

As human beings you wield tremendous power, for you are Creator in human form. Your ability to bear children, to produce art, to compose music and poetry are illustrations of the fact that you are creative beings. You create by thought: your thought is the beginning of your creation and your emotions are your point of attraction for manifesting it. It is the *feeling* you put into your thoughts and ideas that makes them powerful.

Any time you allow a negative encounter to influence your mind or emotions beyond the instant of the actual experience, you therefore have a problem. This is because the energy of the encounter impacts you and serves as a filter which colors future situations. This means that you have effectively handed over your power and you are essentially disclaiming all rights to your own ability to create more positive outcomes.

What more significant travesty is there? For you are here to create: to create learning, to create Understanding, to experience Evolution, to manifest growth. Should you choose not to do so, you are effectively forfeiting the purpose of your life experience and making every difficulty or pain meaningless. You have heard people say, "I don't want all this pain to have been for nothing…" but if you allow your future to be colored by the filters of the past, that is exactly what you are doing.

To not take authority over your inner experience is to forfeit your power as creator. To not take charge over your ability to remove or replace a filter is to rescind your true capacity to create. In so doing you not only surrender your power in shaping your reality, you forfeit your reason for being incarnate.

This is the paramount Truth of human existence. This is why so many lives are being wasted: because they are mis-creating each and every day by relinquishing their power of creation to a television, a friend or relatives. By giving attention and intense emotion to what they do *not* want, countless people are mis-creating the circumstances of their own lives.

Human thought forms the reality of human existence. As you cherish trauma with your television programs spotlighting trauma, trauma shall be yours. As you focus on pain and fear with your newspapers capitalizing on pain and fear, so shall these be yours. And as so many have come to cherish darkness, so too shall that be yours, *en masse*.

But the same is also true of Light. As you cherish joy, joy shall be yours. As you cherish laughter, so shall it be yours. Create a filter of Light which allows all things to look brighter to you. For as you see things in joy, you act in joy; as you act in joy, you create in joy. As you see things with abundance, you act in abundance; as you act from abundance you create abundance. This is how reality is shaped by your filters, thoughts and feelings. It is that simple.

What Color are Your Glasses?

  Imagine it is the holiday of Saint Valentine and you see a big, pink heart in a shop window. You say to yourself, "That pink heart is really pretty and it makes me feel happy. I think I will go purchase a pair of sunglasses with pink lenses so everything I see will be that happy color!" You go to the corner newsstand and do just that. As soon as you put the glasses on, the world takes on a beautiful pink hue no matter where you look.
  Of course, when you have the pink lenses on and you look at the sky, it is not actually pink. You know it only appears that way because you have chosen to see it through your pink filter. You must acknowledge that your view is being affected by the filter of your glasses. As long as you keep those glasses on, you will continue to see the world around you with a pink hue. Also notice there is no prejudice, for everything you cast your gaze upon will be pink, without exception.
  Let us examine how this concept relates to Energy and emotions. Imagine you have had a very fearful experience and

afterward, you are overwhelmed by an urgency not to repeat it. By projecting onto that event an intense repulsion or fear, you are superimposing a powerfully negative filter onto your future. You are placing a filter of darkness, resistance and aversion in front of everything you experience from that moment on, not just repetitions of one specific event.

As such, you will perceive more events as threatening or frightening because of your intense memories of the original fearful encounter. This is not because they are necessarily dangerous or loathsome, but because you are seeing all future situations through that filter. When you are so focused on not wanting to feel such acute anxiety again, everything you experience from that place will be seen through "fear" lenses.

It would be as if you went back to the corner newsstand, but this time you asked to buy a pair of sunglasses with "fear" written across the lenses. From that moment on, everything you encountered would have fear superimposed on it, without exception. Did this happen because you wanted your life to be awful and terrible? No, it is because you made such an emotional investment in your fear it was like you went out and bought "fear" glasses. Be aware that after a while you might not even notice that you still had your "fear" glasses on, but they would continue to color everything you saw, without exception.

This is the power of what is often called "Attraction." In fact it is not so much attraction the way a magnet attracts things, but rather a filter that colors events as if you are wearing glasses.

Now think of how an eye doctor positions his testing machine in front of your face. He turns a small glass lens before your eye and asks, "Can you see more clearly with lens one or two? Can you see more clearly with lens two or three?"

Each time you attach an intense emotion to an experience, the situation itself may end quickly but the filter of your emotional attachment affects everything you see from that moment on. Everything you experience will be colored by that filter until, just like the eye doctor turns the testing lenses, you choose to change your energetic filter. If you do not like Energy one, you go to Energy two; if you don't like Energy two, you go to Energy three.

How does this apply to daily living? Let's say you have an argument with your significant other and you do not like the way you are feeling. Being mindful of your Energy, you decide to try to enhance your inner condition for the mutual benefit of all. In order to change your Energy lens, you decide to take a shower to clear your head. If you find taking a shower is not enough to change your lens, you should then try going to another part of the house and if that is not enough, put in a movie…

It is important that you not give up but keep trying until you can change your filter to something that is peaceful, calm or compassionate. Clearing your Energy should be the priority until the negative filter is removed; do whatever you can to get out of that space.

By doing so, you save yourself the struggle of experiencing that energy the next time you encounter a difficult person or circumstance. With practice, you can learn to take power over your Energy and enjoy seeing your life through the lenses of Peace, Understanding and Light.

Embracing Winter

Winter is arriving and you are sad about that. I can hear it every day when you come to Me for wisdom: complaining, complaining. But you are small in your spirit when you see the world in that way, and when you complain about the Natural Order of things you reveal your immaturity.

Winter is a time of profound and powerful Energy. You do not feel it because you perceive it from a place of judgment. But *I* see it because I am big in My view and I can sense what is happening. It would be wise for you to look at winter from a more spiritual perspective this year. Pay attention to what is transpiring within the Earth's Energy at such times of rest.

When the Earth is blanketed and there is nothing to look at, there is only one place to turn. That place is within your heart. Your complaining simply shows that you do not understand what it means to turn away from the distractions of the man-made world and enter the quiet inner realm of the heart. If you would consider this as you prepare for the coming season of introspection, you could view winter from a place of Higher Understanding.

As you experience times of natural darkness and the Sun is less present remember, too, that not all light is equal. The radiance of a flame is going to have superior Energy to the glow of electricity. If you are feeling a sense of loss in your spirit for the presence of light, do not just turn on all the lamps in your home. You need to introduce natural Energy by lighting candles or warm fires in the hearth, as well.

For it is the *Energy* that you are really missing, not just the presence of visual light. You are craving the Energy that the Sun represents and flame resembles it most closely, simply on a smaller scale. Lighting candles during seasons of darkness can create an enormous shift and help uplift your spirit until Nature's cycle leads you again to the radiance of spring.

Lessons from the Land

There are many ways to benefit from the landscape you call your life. To appreciate it, keep your eyes open for the subtle lessons and tiny joys sprinkled throughout it like feathers in the grass as you walk. Enjoy the fact that today the mist rolled back and the Sun appeared. Take pleasure in the pheasants who took flight as you passed and delight in the tiny frog which leapt from the side of the pond into the water.

Open yourself to the presence of those who share the day with you. Learn from your puppy how to play and rest, to sit on a hill and open to the Sun. Discover the pleasure of lying back and enjoying a peaceful day spent quietly together. Follow her example and delight in stretching your muscles and feeling your body come alive.

As you spend time in quiet reflection, look for the lessons hidden in the landscape itself: lessons of changing seasons, of sinking your roots deep, the power of rest. These are the important principles you will see played out in the most powerful moments of your life, often in the form of relationship or health challenges.

Remember to notice the Sky above you, too. The Sky could be compared to the spiritual experience of your life. It is subtle, ever-present, easily missed and often ignored until It forces you to pay attention, as when the Sky opens to release a downpour upon the land.

Just as you seldom pause to notice the Sky above you, you rarely take time to experience yourself as a spiritual being for more than an hour each day. Why is that? Just as the Sky yields special blessings, the spirit realm offers unique gifts, too. And the lessons it provides are the lessons of the soul, which are the most important of all.

Begin to interact with spiritual Energy more often, even when there is nothing urgent you need. Pause to simply sit with Goodness in the peaceful manner you have learned from your puppy. When you Commune with the spiritual Energy of the Universe, there is no need to go anywhere or do anything. Rather, you can quietly enjoy the Sun on your face, contentment in your heart and the benefit of true, spiritual Communion.

Raise Your Spear

    You must *try* in your life. You must be brave. You must step forward and not be stopped because you feel afraid. Like a young Indian warrior learning to hunt, you must raise your spear with courage and thrust it at the life that would be your prize.
    Sometimes you will fear that it will cost you everything. There will be moments when you are afraid that the buffalo will trample you or the mountain lion will tear you apart with its claws and sometimes, there is no way to know that they will not. Sometimes you just step forth and prepare to throw your spear. You do not have a promise of success, you do not know if you will die today. But you step up anyway, and you try.
    I believe that in your older age you have lost some of your courage, so you must reclaim your bravery now. You must find the boldness of youth again. Do not be afraid to test, to try, to risk the conveniences and comforts of your life for those things which matter most.

To find your courage you must go inside and dig it up like a bear digs up a clam. As you do so, you will begin to feel strong again. But remember: You cannot be strong without trying. You must do those things which make you tremble, and in so doing you will find the key to your power and success.

Go into your life unmoved and unhindered by your own fear. Challenge yourself to step up to the fight and hold your spear high, even if your arm is trembling. Do not be afraid of your fear. Do not be stopped by your shaking. For in the end, whether your trophy was won in bravery or it was won in fear, it is the same celebration. Whether you come home having been courageous or you come home having shaken in your shoes, you still get to carry the prize!

Do not let your fear stop you. Do not let doubt hold you back. This is the way of the warrior and this is what you have come—and *who* you have come—to be.

From Trying to Success

    As you lift your gaze to the Sky, you see above you a big yellow balloon. In it are people who hang in a basket far above the surface of the Earth. They have chosen to experience the joy that is a view of the planet from above, even though it is an awesome and daunting task. How many will look up at them today and say, "Ah, I would love to do that!" Yet, how few shall ever find the courage to reach up and touch the Sky.
    Living life to the fullest is likewise a rarely-claimed prize. Not many are willing to imagine their Highest Truth and even fewer fulfill It. But for one within whom the heart is humble and the reward is cherished, the Highest Truth can be achieved.
    Without commitment and dedication you cannot fulfill your Highest Purpose. It is true that you do not have a promise of success, but you step up anyway and you try. In that trying comes learning, and from learning comes knowing, and from knowing comes doing, and from doing comes success.

If you live in this way you can claim the reward of your Destiny. Even if your hand trembles at the awesomeness of a challenging task, you will find that somewhere within you lies the heart of a warrior. In the important moment of opportunity you will be able to follow through and claim the treasure of your life's Purpose.

Such things do not happen by mistake, for to be courageous requires trying and doing again and again. Not many are willing to try, and even fewer are willing to do again and again that which they must in order to find success. But there is no other way to claim your prize and live your Highest Truth.

Make no mistake—there are no second chances. This is your one life like this and there will not be another like it. Do not give yourself the excuse of saying, "Some say there are many lifetimes, so I will take it easy and be comfortable in this one." No, *this* life matters now and you must do your best in each one. You cannot trade it off, saying that there will be other chances.

It is time for you to stop being afraid and to claim your Destiny. As you do so, you will find that your trying becomes success and your fear has fallen away. But such things do not come easily and they are not in one day won. It takes time. It takes practice. You must go out into the valley again and again and try, with your spear, to hunt the life which is your prey. You must try, in your fear, to stand tall and claim your Destiny. And in that trying you will find success.

Shedding Your Spiritual Skin

    The spiritual Journey is an Evolution, a natural releasing of the old for the new like a snake shedding its skin. In spiritual transformation, there must be a willingness to lay down that which is no longer fully a part of you. This process of releasing takes place whether you believe a transformation was your idea or not, and whether you feel you are prepared for it or not. At some point you must relinquish the old, which is often holding only by a thread to you, so that you can be free to move about and fully live.
    Depending on the circumstances, shedding your spiritual skin can take minutes, hours, days, even years. But mark these words: The pace of releasing the past does not depend on the depth of love in any relationship or circumstance. Instead, it depends on one's *attachment* to the past and one's level of spiritual maturity. Even those whom you dearly love, for whom you would gladly lay down your own life, may be set free with respectful surrender. But this

can only happen if you are able to release your attachment to the old and cultivate enough spiritual maturity to welcome the new.

When you move into a season of change with a heart of Understanding, the transition can be smooth and natural. It may not be comfortable—as shedding a skin is not comfortable—it may not be quick—as shedding a skin is not quick—but it can be natural and smooth. The more you surrender yourself to the process, the more efficiently the process can unfold.

So it is in your best interest, whether you believe you chose a change or it happened without your expectation, to flow with the shift as best you can. In this way you most expeditiously transform your life and release the Energy that is no longer a part of your reality, no matter how much you wish It to be. Anything that is no longer within your current reality needs to be released so you can move ahead and grow.

Depending on your Understanding and level of attachment, transitioning from old to new can take a short or long period of time. It is up to each of you to decide if you will resist the transformation or if you will rise up and claim the new, gracefully surrendering what has been for all you may become.

Receive Blessings with Grace

    The life you are here to live is not one of sadness but one of joy. At times, you will find yourself challenged to remain joyful while others try to rob you of your delight. In their cynicism or bitterness, some may cast doubt upon what you have worked hard to create. They will try to steal the contentment that is rightfully yours. But you must not let them do so, for you have earned your happiness and others do not deserve to take it from you.
    Everything around and about you is there by right. Every bit of joy, every bit of satisfaction—these things have come not by *luck* but through your own good work as you strive toward Truth and Light. Each time a blessing comes to you, accept it as your rightful gift, for it is something which you have paid for and has been justly earned.
    Imagine if you were to purchase an item of loveliness but when it was delivered to you, you rejected it saying, "That is not mine." What you have paid for is yours in rights and belongs to

you. Do not reject the delight and happiness which are so truly and clearly yours.

Many people are unsure when they encounter blessings if they should reach out and claim them. This is the sad evidence of spirituality gone wrong, a spirituality which has told its people they are not worthy to receive. Such a philosophy says if a blessing comes your way that you must be on guard, for it may be a trick. It may be a test instead of a reward for your good spiritual work.

Yet there is, somewhere within you, the grace and the courage to receive. Such things are not easily won, and for many people it is difficult to accept even the joys which are rightfully theirs. But it is possible to learn to receive blessings, and if you will give thanks for each one as it comes you will begin to draw more and more goodness into your life.

The Value of Spiritual Practice

Sometimes you wonder to yourself, "Of what merit is it if I spend all my time in mediation and do nothing but sit in stillness hour after hour? True, it is spiritual Communion but what purpose does it serve?" I shall tell you now.

On the one hand, your gift of a positive vibration uplifts the larger whole of the Universe. Your Energy cannot be divorced from the Energy of all beings, both human and non-human, who surround you. Every time you choose to follow the Path of Light, you help the whole of the Universe maintain Its resonance with Truth.

On the other hand, if you possess the gift of positive Energy and you do *not* give it, you have chosen to enhance the darkness that is a part of All That Is. Although both Light and darkness are natural parts of the purity that is Allness, they have different consequences for the world and people around you. If you wish to see others uplifted and hopeful, it matters greatly that you choose a Path of Light in all your actions.

You see before you clouds that change and move just as you have watched them change and move every day. You also see before you a landscape which does not appear to move and feels solid beneath your feet. Yet beyond your perception the land does move, and you feel the effects of those movements when they manifest as seasonal changes and storms.

Every day you are making choices in favor of Light or dark. Just as the Earth's changes are sometimes visible to you and sometimes not, you may think that your choices are unknown to those around you. But every choice you make affects the larger whole, contributing to the *flow* that is inherent in the Universe. For in the constant dance that is Universal Reality, flow is required for Energy to exist in purity.

If you desire that all should live in Peace and Truth, you must recognize that your life should be one of service to Light. You must cherish what you know to be Truth and share It with others. Do not discriminate with whom you will share your Light based on another's appearance. For who can say which person will see your example and choose rightly in the end? It is not always the man who has the longest robe and the pride of a zealot. It is sometimes the pauper, who decides beyond his own self-interest to care for another whose life he values above his own.

So do not think your actions, including those performed in solitude, matter not. Every day your Energy affects the reality of those near you, and you must be diligent in your adherence to Truth if you wish to see the world around renewed and transformed.

A Blessed Holiday Season

As your Guides, We would like you to approach the holidays you celebrate differently this year. Encourage others to see this season as a time for gratitude, not a time for drama. When you give gifts to others, you may wish to include a little note with a heartfelt wish or blessing for each of your loved ones. You could each take turns saying a bit about what another person means to you. Buy gifts if you want, but also plan to give a little something extra others did not expect. And remember, regardless of spiritual differences, everyone on your planet can celebrate the Solstice to honor the Energy of Light.

You have been told that the winter season is one of turning inward, but that does not mean it is easy to ignore the darkened, wintry landscape around you. To deny your feelings of loss regarding the diminished amount of light or warmth is to keep yourself stuck in resistance. Honor but release your sadness by having a ceremony celebrating the warmer seasons which have passed. Paying homage to the Sun or flowers, as with Solstice celebrations, is one way to offer gratitude for such gifts and keep them close to your heart.

By acknowledging the hibernating beauty in the outer world, you are thereby free to move toward the beauty within. This ushers you into the mystical winter months wherein you can practice more quiet meditation and peaceful contemplation, as all things in Nature are doing.

Winter is a time for storytelling, it is a time of fires and warmth. For the people who once roamed upon this land, winter was a season for warm blankets wrapped around oneself, a time of family gathering together and being close instead of spread out across the land.

Look at this holiday season in a way you never have before and cherish that what is rich, sweet and nourishing. You need more light in your life during the period around the Solstice, so build a fire or ritualistically light candles to help replace the light which has been lost.

There is a sweetness and a freshness that is lacking in winter as well, and you can supplement these with the foods you eat. Savor the tanginess of pineapple, the freshness of lemons and citrus, the sweetness of candied fruits. All of these are part of the lightness of a Sun Season and difficult to find in a winter or Moon Season.

Begin to see with new eyes this time of year and how to bring to it a unique and blessed quality. Welcome into your heart the uplifting Light of the spirit and share It with others, even in the midst of winter.

Ask for Help to Help Yourself

So much of what you need lies within your own heart if you will but open yourself up to it. You can find, in the quietness of private moments, that healing and Peace for which you so earnestly long if you will simply ask for Our help. Just as your little puppy begs to be picked up by putting her tiny paws on your leg, you likewise lift your heart to Us when you need comfort. In those moments, We gladly reach down and hold you, cradling you close within Our loving Energy.

There will be times of difficulty and challenge in your life, times when you will find yourself unwilling to go on. It is in such moments that you must reach for Us and We will gladly and mercifully sustain you. You hold much power and courage within your heart, but you do not yet hold everything. You have not yet found constant bliss and Peace or complete courage in the face of difficulty, but you do *have the tools to find these* when need be. Such tools include the ability to ask, the ability to seek and the ability to draw Us close to you.

With these tools you feed and heal your own soul. Although a self-judging part of you may consider such assistance to be "another doing it for you," you are actually healing yourself. Do not look down upon asking for help as escapism or as you not doing your own spiritual work. Rather, see the practice of asking Us for help as you helping yourself and becoming aware that what you need is within your reach.

We reside as close as your own breath and, therefore, you do not have to ask for another person's permission to find Peace. You do not have to go to a special location or follow someone else's prescription for happiness. You can find yourself at Peace any time in any place, simply by calling Our name and allowing Our healing Energy to flow into your heart.

Opening to What May Be

  Many things in your life have changed over the past year. Whether joyful or challenging, these changes are to be commended for they are all part of your spiritual growth. Yet, there is one change that is more important than all the rest and it is the practice of having an open and loving heart. Sensitivity to Our Presence, Compassion toward others and gratitude for your blessings are all evidence of an open-hearted spirit.
  What you are visioning for your future will come at some price, but there will be moments that are so fulfilling, any price will be worth paying. Spend your Energy wisely. Those things which bring joy or a sense of Peace and clarity are worthy of pursuing. Activities which invite fear, incite competition or create frustration are not worthy of your Energy.
  There is an animated movie in which a mouse father tries earnestly to convince his unusually courageous son to become more fearful the way a proper mouse should. The father exclaims,

"There are so many wonderful things in the world to be afraid of, if you are just willing to see how scary they really are!"

Sometimes people who are afraid try to instill their fears within your heart. Does this make them your fears? No, they belong to someone else. Part of your spiritual work is to keep a sense of separation between you and those who live in fear, anger or limitation. You must learn to live your joyful life and not be drawn down by those who dwell in negativity.

Everything of Light that you dream about can be a part of your future. It may not come easily, it will not appear instantly, but it can be yours. It is important for you to keep your desire to create positive Energy very strong. Then you can attract things which suit you, which open your heart and help you achieve the level of fulfillment you can surely attain.

Remember that change comes slowly in Nature and it allows things time to adjust to what they are becoming. Just as a butterfly must take time to emerge from the cocoon so, too, must you take time to prepare for a new phase of life in the coming year. If you will grow slowly and thoughtfully you will not emerge with malformed parts, unprepared for the journey ahead. Instead, you will be completely mature in all your talents and Energies, ready to enjoy the life you are meant to lead. Every part of you will be primed to receive more Light and joy as you grow into a new year of opportunity and becoming.

ABOUT THE AUTHOR

     L. Taylor is a spiritual consultant and clairaudient who loves music, reading and nurturing the plants in her desert home. She considers daily time in Nature essential to her sense of well-being. Her greatest delight is using her spiritual gifts to help others find their innermost Truth.

     Ms. Taylor resides in Sedona, Arizona where she shares a home with her husband and their beloved dog, for whom she enjoys knitting tiny sweaters.